This book

belongs to

....

....

Written by Gaby Goldsack
Photography by Martin Haswell
With special thanks to Stonar School

This is a Parragon Publishing book
This edition published 2006

Parragon
Queen Street House
4 Queen Street
Bath BA1 1HE, UK

ISBN 1-40547-070-4
Printed in China

Horses and Ponies

p

Contents

Horses and ponies

Horses and ponies belong to the horse family. Small horses measuring up to 14.2 hands (about 5 feet) high at the shoulder are called ponies. Anything taller is a horse.

> **Horses and ponies are measured in hands. A hand is 4 inches (or 10 centimetres).**

There are many words to describe a horse or pony according to how old it is and whether it is male or female.

A **foal** is a baby horse up to 1 year old.

A **colt** is a male horse up to 3 years old.

A **dam** is a mother horse.

A **filly** is a female horse up to 3 years old.

A **mare** is a female horse more than 4 years old.

A **gelding** is a male horse that has been gelded. This means it cannot breed (make babies).

A **stallion** is a male horse more than 3 years old that can breed.

Shetland

The Shetland pony is ideal for small children. Although it is under 10.2 hands hands, it is very strong.

Thoroughbred

The thoroughbred is the fastest horse in the world. Most racehorses are thoroughbred.

Shire

The Shire (a type of draft horse) is the tallest horse in the world. It can grow to more than 18 hands high.

Colors and markings

Horses and ponies come in many different colors. They also have different markings that help you tell one from another.

Black
Black ponies have a black coat, mane, and tail.

Brown
A brown pony has a mixture of brown and black hairs covering its body.

Bay
A bay has a brown body with a black mane, tail, and legs.

Chestnut

A chestnut has an orange-colored body. The mane and tail are usually a similar color.

Skewbald

A skewbald has brown and white patches. A piebald has black and white patches.

Gray

A pony is called a gray when it is gray or white.

star   *blaze*   *sock*   *stocking*

Horse and pony points

The parts of a horse or pony's body are called its points. It's a good idea to know these.

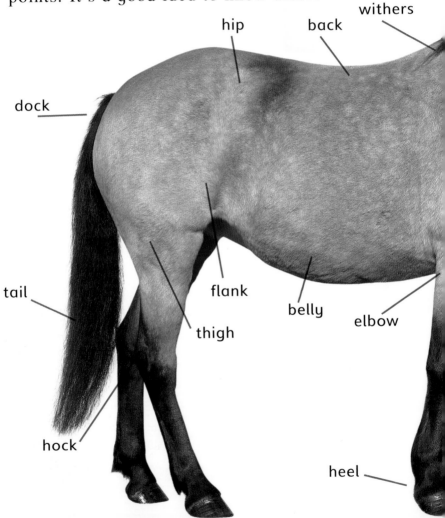

hip

back

withers

dock

tail

hock

flank

thigh

belly

elbow

heel

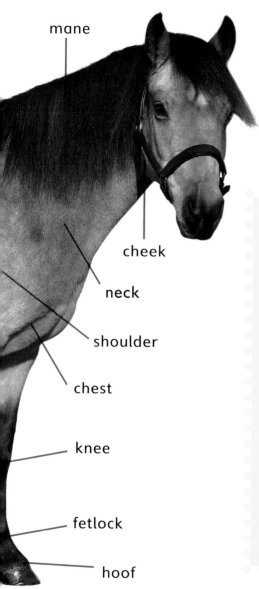

mane

cheek

neck

shoulder

chest

knee

fetlock

hoof

The hoof

A horse's foot is called a hoof. The outside of the hoof is made of horn. The horn grows all the time, like your fingernails.

Catching your pony

Never creep up behind a horse or pony—you might startle it and make it kick out. Let it know you are coming by saying hello and approaching from the side. Let it sniff your hand and give it a rub on the neck.

Approach the pony on its left (near) side.

Walk beside the pony's neck as you lead it.

Quick-release knot

Use a quick-release knot to tie up a pony. That way, it can be released quickly in an emergency. Tie the rope to a piece of string attached to a metal ring. The string will break if the pony pulls back in fright and stop it from hurting itself or damaging property.

1. Push the rope through the string and make a loop in the rope.

2. Make another loop in the end of the rope and pull it through the first loop.

3. To undo the knot quickly, simply pull on the free end.

Tacking up

The horse or pony wears a saddle and a bridle for riding. This is called the tack.

1. Hold the saddle on your left arm with the pommel (front) near the crook of your elbow.

2. Lift the saddle onto the pony's back, just in front of its withers. Slide the saddle back into position.

3. Let down the girth and bring it under the pony's tummy. Buckle the girth to the straps underneath the saddle flap.

1. Loop the reins over the pony's neck. Put the bridle over the pony's nose. Slide the bit into its mouth.

2. Lift the top of the bridle over its ears.

3. Fasten the throat latch and noseband.

What to wear

You will need to wear special clothes to ride safely and comfortably. You should always wear a properly fitted riding hat to protect your head in case you fall off.

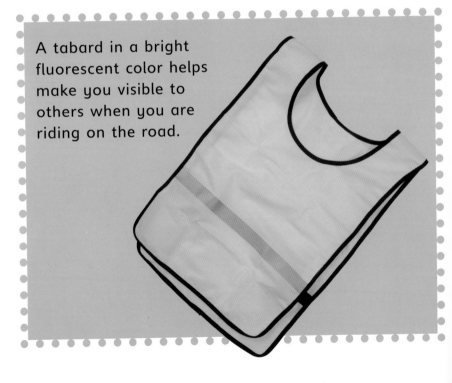

A tabard in a bright fluorescent color helps make you visible to others when you are riding on the road.

Your **hat** should always be fastened under the chin.

A **body protector** will protect your spine, shoulders, and organs if you take a tumble.

Riding gloves have grips on the palms to stop the reins from slipping through your fingers.

Riding breeches are stretchy and make riding more comfortable.

A **crop** is used only if your pony ignores your signals. It should never be used in anger.

Jodhpur boots are short and made from leather.

Getting on and off

Getting on your horse or pony is called mounting. Before mounting, check that the girth is tight enough. You should be able to fit two fingers under the girth. If it is loose, tighten the buckles under the saddle flap.

1. With the reins in your left hand, put your left foot in the stirrup.

2. Hold the saddle with your right hand and push off the ground. Swing your right leg over the pony's back.

3. Put your right foot into the stirrup and hold your reins in both hands.

1. To dismount take both feet out of your stirrups and put both reins in your left hand.

2. Resting both hands on the front of the saddle, lean forward and swing your right leg over the pony's back.

3. With knees bent, drop to the ground.

To check that your stirrups are the right length, let your legs hang down out of the stirrups. The bottom of the stirrup should be level with your ankle.

Sitting

The way you sit on a
horse or pony is called
your position. A well
balanced position will
help you stay safe in
your seat.

Look in the
direction you
are going.

Don't grip with
your knees.

Rest the balls of your
feet in the stirrups.
Keep your heels down.

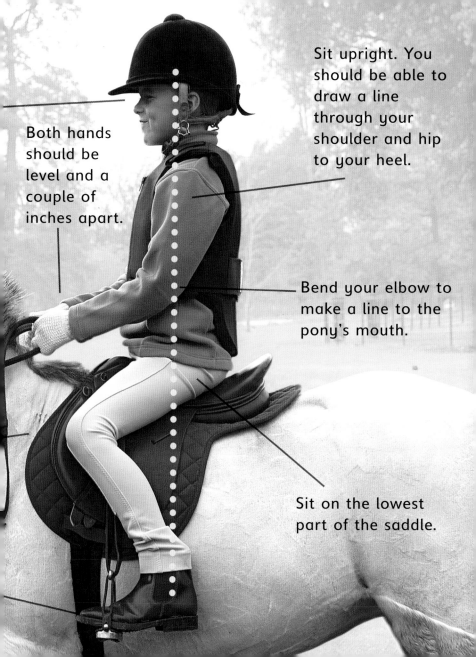

Both hands should be level and a couple of inches apart.

Sit upright. You should be able to draw a line through your shoulder and hip to your heel.

Bend your elbow to make a line to the pony's mouth.

Sit on the lowest part of the saddle.

Walking and trotting

To get a horse or pony moving you have to use your legs, hands, body, and voice. These are called the aids.

Ask your pony to walk forward by squeezing with both legs. Let your hands follow the movement of the pony's head.

To turn left, look left, move your right leg behind the girth and squeeze with both legs. At the same time, squeeze the left rein and give with your right rein. To turn right, do the opposite.

Before asking your pony to trot, shorten the reins. Then squeeze with both legs. This is a sitting trot.

For a rising trot push into the stirrups so that your bottom is lifted out of the saddle on one beat, then gently sit back down on the next. Repeat "up, down, up, down" in your head.

Ask your pony to stop by gently squeezing the reins so that it feels like pulling against strong elastic.

Cantering and galloping

You can start to canter from a trot. To do this,
stop rising and sit for a few strides. Then
brush your outside leg back behind the girth.
At the same time squeeze with your inside
leg. Sit well down in the saddle
and rock with the rhythm
of the canter.

Outside leg

Inside leg

To ask your pony to go into a gallop from a canter, squeeze with both legs. Then shift your weight forward out of the saddle and push your hands up the pony's neck.

Getting ready to jump

Before taking your pony over a small jump, practice your jumping position.

Keep your chin up and look forward between the pony's ears.

Keep your back flat.

Fold forward from the hip and slide your bottom backward.

Your knees should rest against the saddle.

Push more weight into your heels. This will stop you from catapulting over the pony's head if it refuses at a jump, or stops sudddenly, or swerves.

Shorten your stirrups by a hole or two.

Shorten your reins.

Walk around the paddock in the jumping position. When you feel ready, move onto a trot. Keep this position as you ride over one pole.

Now try three poles 4–4ft 6in (1.2–1.3m) apart. As the pony stretches its neck out over the poles, push your hands forward so that you don't hold him back.

Jumping

Once you are happy with your jumping position, you should be ready to jump a small fence. There are five stages to the jump: approach, takeoff, suspension, landing, and getaway.

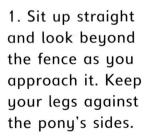

1. Sit up straight and look beyond the fence as you approach it. Keep your legs against the pony's sides.

2. Bend at the hips and push your weight into your heels. Move your hands up toward the pony's ears.

3. Look straight ahead as you fly over the fence.

Crosspole jump

Upright jump

Spread jump

4. Sit up and look in the direction you want to go. Try not to thump into the saddle.

5. Sit up and bring your hands back without pulling at the reins.

Grooming

Horses and ponies need regular cleaning to stay healthy and tidy. This is called grooming.

Using a face brush, brush the pony's hairs in the direction they grow.

Use a wide brush to remove mud from the pony's body especially where the saddle and bridle will sit.

Pick out hay and tangles from the mane and tail with your fingers. Then brush one section at a time with a body brush.

Pick up the pony's hoof, and use a hoof pick to clean it out. The sharp point of the hoof pick should point toward the toe.

Feeding

Ponies can be fed many different types of food. Ask an expert what you should feed your pony.

Hay is dried grass.

When feeding from your hand, hold your palm flat with your thumbs tucked out of the way.

Nuts or **cubes** are pellets of dried food.

Ponies need clean drinking water.

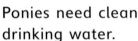

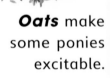

Oats make some ponies excitable.

Cut apples and carrots into chunks so that your pony doesn't choke on them.